I0397196

Client Log

This log belongs to

Clients Name	Appointment Date	Appointment Time	Paid/Owed

Notes

Clients Name	Appointment Date	Appointment Time	Paid/Owed

Notes

Clients Name	Appointment Date	Appointment Time	Paid / Owed

Notes

Clients Name	Appointment Date	Appointment Time	Paid/Owed

Notes

Clients Name	Appointment Date	Appointment Time	Paid/Owed

Notes

Clients Name	Appointment Date	Appointment Time	Paid / Owed

Notes

Clients Name	Appointment Date	Appointment Time	Paid / Owed

Notes

Clients Name	Appointment Date	Appointment Time	Paid/Owed

Notes

Clients Name	Appointment Date	Appointment Time	Paid/Owed

Notes

Clients Name	Appointment Date	Appointment Time	Paid/Owed

Notes

Clients Name	Appointment Date	Appointment Time	Paid/Owed

Notes

Clients Name	Appointment Date	Appointment Time	Paid/Owed

Notes

Clients Name	Appointment Date	Appointment Time	Paid/Owed

Notes

Clients Name	Appointment Date	Appointment Time	Paid/Owed

Notes

Clients Name	Appointment Date	Appointment Time	Paid/Owed

Notes

Clients Name	Appointment Date	Appointment Time	Paid/Owed

Notes

Clients Name	Appointment Date	Appointment Time	Paid/Owed

Notes

Clients Name	Appointment Date	Appointment Time	Paid/Owed

Notes

Clients Name	Appointment Date	Appointment Time	Paid/Owed

Notes

Clients Name	Appointment Date	Appointment Time	Paid/Owed

Notes

Clients Name	Appointment Date	Appointment Time	Paid / Owed

Notes

Clients Name	Appointment Date	Appointment Time	Paid/Owed

Notes

Clients Name	Appointment Date	Appointment Time	Paid/Owed

Notes

Clients Name	Appointment Date	Appointment Time	Paid/Owed

Notes

Clients Name	Appointment Date	Appointment Time	Paid/Owed

Notes

Clients Name	Appointment Date	Appointment Time	Paid/Owed

Notes

Clients Name	Appointment Date	Appointment Time	Paid/Owed

Notes

Clients Name	Appointment Date	Appointment Time	Paid/Owed

Notes

Clients Name	Appointment Date	Appointment Time	Paid/Owed

Notes

Clients Name	Appointment Date	Appointment Time	Paid / Owed

Notes

Clients Name	Appointment Date	Appointment Time	Paid/Owed

Notes

Clients Name	Appointment Date	Appointment Time	Paid/Owed

Notes

Clients Name	Appointment Date	Appointment Time	Paid/Owed

Notes

Clients Name	Appointment Date	Appointment Time	Paid/Owed

Notes

Clients Name	Appointment Date	Appointment Time	Paid/Owed

Notes

Clients Name	Appointment Date	Appointment Time	Paid / Owed

Notes

Clients Name	Appointment Date	Appointment Time	Paid/Owed

Notes

Clients Name	Appointment Date	Appointment Time	Paid/Owed

Notes

Clients Name	Appointment Date	Appointment Time	Paid/Owed

Notes

Clients Name	Appointment Date	Appointment Time	Paid/Owed

Notes

Clients Name	Appointment Date	Appointment Time	Paid/Owed

Notes

Clients Name	Appointment Date	Appointment Time	Paid/Owed

Notes

Clients Name	Appointment Date	Appointment Time	Paid/Owed

Notes

Clients Name	Appointment Date	Appointment Time	Paid/Owed

Notes

Clients Name	Appointment Date	Appointment Time	Paid / Owed

Notes

Clients Name	Appointment Date	Appointment Time	Paid/Owed

Notes

Clients Name	Appointment Date	Appointment Time	Paid/Owed

Notes

Clients Name	Appointment Date	Appointment Time	Paid/Owed

Notes

Clients Name	Appointment Date	Appointment Time	Paid/Owed

Notes

Clients Name	Appointment Date	Appointment Time	Paid/Owed

Notes

Clients Name	Appointment Date	Appointment Time	Paid / Owed

Notes

Clients Name	Appointment Date	Appointment Time	Paid/Owed

Notes

Clients Name	Appointment Date	Appointment Time	Paid/Owed

Notes

Clients Name	Appointment Date	Appointment Time	Paid/Owed

Notes

Clients Name	Appointment Date	Appointment Time	Paid/Owed

Notes

Clients Name	Appointment Date	Appointment Time	Paid/Owed

Notes

Clients Name	Appointment Date	Appointment Time	Paid/Owed

Notes

Clients Name	Appointment Date	Appointment Time	Paid/Owed

Notes

Clients Name	Appointment Date	Appointment Time	Paid/Owed

Notes

Clients Name	Appointment Date	Appointment Time	Paid / Owed

www.ingramcontent.com/pod-product-compliance
Lightning Source LLC
Chambersburg PA
CBHW072213170526
45158CB00002BA/579